A FINANCIAL ANALYSIS OF RISK AND CONTROL

Applying Financial Analysis to Improve Risk and Control Decision Making

ROD SMITH

outskirts
press

Table of Contents

CHAPTER 1

Background

I have spent most of my career in the risk-and-control profession, for the most part as an external auditor assessing the design and operating effectiveness of controls, primarily information technology. Over this period, I have witnessed remarkable growth in the profession in terms of its significance, the general level of practice and the standards employed. While the practice of the risk-and-control profession has grown in sophistication over time, I believe there are a couple aspects of current practice and decision-making that are a bit crude and inconsistent with sound management decision-making and business analysis. The foremost of these is the economic evaluation of controls. It is my observation that methods routinely used when evaluating business decisions from an economic standpoint are either not employed or are used to a much lesser extent in the risk-and-control realm. Indeed, many organizations seem to view the effort to implement an effective control environment to be a "necessary evil" or a "cost of doing business" and therefore the subject does not command the degree of analysis and evaluation that is afforded other business decisions where the organization has more freedom to accept or reject a proposed investment. Many organizations, furthermore, view achieving a sound control environment as an imperative, requiring whatever investment is deemed necessary. For this and other similar reasons, the prevailing attitude seems to be that the financial implications of controls are relatively immaterial, given the view that these costs are unavoidable, and an organization cannot realize significant benefits from evaluating its investment in controls. Furthermore, to the extent that the financial implications are considered, they are evaluated in a manner that reflects this underlying view and bias—that the control environment should be afforded only the resources, capital, and analysis required to attain basic compliance with applicable regulatory requirements or to achieve a control environment that is deemed minimally acceptable to external auditors and other interested parties.

On the other hand, other organizations seem to view control objectives and regulatory requirements too literally, implementing general recommendations uncritically and largely without regard for, or measurement of, the underlying control exposure or the associated implementation and operating costs. There are several reasons for the lack of financial discipline in the risk and control profession, however, this behavior seems counter-productive, given the scale of resources and capital spent on designing, implementing and operating their system of controls, as well as the cost of ongoing assessment of controls and the control environment.

As a discipline, the risk-and-control profession appears to foster an insensitivity to economic considerations. At times it seems as though the qualities needed to be an effective risk-and-control professional in some respects promotes this point of view and behavior. For example, objectivity and independence, the qualities of being psychologically and organizationally removed from the control area(s) being assessed, may cultivate a mentality that will submit control recommendations with little regard for their practicality in terms of operational efficiency and cost. Ultimately, this may result in an expensive and inefficient control environment. The objective of this book is to demonstrate that, despite the fundamental differences inherent to the risk-and-control area, it should warrant the same degree of rigor and discipline in terms of financial and operational analysis as is applied to other topics of comparable cost, scale and complexity. After establishing this point, the text will outline a rudimentary framework for evaluating controls from a financial standpoint that can be applied in a manner consistent with financial analysis of other areas of the organization but which is tailored to the needs of the risk-and-control discipline. Last, the implications of applying such a framework to all aspects of the realm of risk and control (e.g., the design, implementation, operation, and assessment of controls) will be considered in order to understand, at least "directionally", the guidelines and considerations for applying financial analysis to controls to reduce costs and increase the efficiency and effectiveness of an organization's control environment. In summary, it is hoped that this work will assist organizations in maximizing the return on their sizable investment in the design, implementation, operation, and ongoing assessment of their control environment.

CHAPTER 2

A Financial Definition Of Control

Prior to outlining a framework for analyzing control from a financial/economic standpoint, it will be helpful to develop a basic definition of control that lends itself to financial analysis and which also distinguishes the subject matter from other business activities. Before we develop a definition of controls that suits this purpose, let us first outline a general definition of a business objective, or more broadly, an organizational activity or objective.

Definition of a Business Activity/Organizational Objective [from a financial perspective]

For the purposes of financial analysis, an organizational activity can be defined as follows:

> *The commitment of scarce resources (capital, labor, and/or materials) required to achieve intended favorable outcomes (such as the production of goods and rendering of services) that achieves (or supports the achievement of) a positive financial return.*

I understand that defining the goal of all business activities and organization objectives in strictly financial terms may be unsatisfactory to many readers, as it seems too narrow and mercenary. It is, however, an appropriate definition for the purpose of examining a financial analysis of risk and controls. It is certainly true that not all business activity is undertaken to yield a positive and tangible economic return—for example, many business activities are undertaken for altruistic reasons, such as charity or community relations, (although one could reasonably assert that there are significant economic benefits associated with the goodwill and reputational gain that accrues to an organization from these activities). However, for the sake of this analysis, we will concentrate on the broad range of activities that are driven, at least in part, by financial considerations, which is the fundamental and overarching principle in a market-based, or, for that matter, any other efficiency- or utility-optimizing model for decision-making, whereby economic gain is the most useful and uniformly applicable motivation and measure of results that can be applied to most decision-making contexts.

Figure 1, below, provides some examples of organizational activities outlining the components of the definition above.

Activity/ Objective	Description	Comments
Launching a new product line	Completing the research, design, manufacturing, marketing, and logistics necessary to launch a new product line.	Requires a large commitment of employees, intellectual property, and financial resources. If successful, the resulting product line should provide a revenue stream in excess of the commitment of resources (costs) – a positive return on investment (ROI).

Activity/ Objective	Description	Comments
Implementing a new system	Design and implementation of a system that allows its users to work more quickly and accurately and to provide superior customer service or otherwise render additional services or improved product utility/quality.	Requires the commitment of salaried employees, information systems hardware, and software to develop a new system.
Implementing and operating a training program	Development of training content and presentation material as well as delivery of training.	Requires significant internal staffing and possibly external consultants to develop the training material and to present and deliver the content.
Running payroll	The capture of employee time charges to be used as input, the loading of the payroll roster, and execution of the payroll cycle.	Requires the time and effort of properly trained employees to run the payroll cycle. If executed correctly, only authorized employees will receive pay, and their payment(s) will be received timely, in the correct amount, with the proper tax withholding and other deductions. Requires the expenditure of some effort and time to set up the payroll and run and review output reports to ensure that it was processed correctly. In addition to the costs expended in executing and performing this activity, incorrect payroll processing can result in significant cleanup expenses and other liabilities.

Activity/ Objective	Description	Comments
Posting a manual general ledger (G/L) entry	Preparing and posting a manual G/L entry, including any authorizations that may be necessary.	Involves the proper preparation of supporting documentation and identification of the correct accounts to which to post the entries (debit and credits). May also require supervisory review and/or approval. Improper or erroneous processing comes with significant costs, including increased internal financial reporting and external audit fees.

The Common Characteristics of Business Activities

As you can see from **Figure 1** above, the wide range of business activities described have certain common traits. That is, each activity has the following characteristics:

- Completion of the activity requires an expenditure of economic resources (capital, labor and/or materials).
- Successful completion of the activity yields a positive economic benefit (which may be difficult to define and measure.)

These characteristics are the positive or direct economic costs and benefits of undertaking these business objectives/activities. Let's term them the "affirmative economic costs and benefits" of business activities.

Likewise, in an inverse sense, business activities can also yield (unintended) 'negative' economic costs and benefits, for example, in **Figure 1**, above, we outline some of the consequences and costs if the prescribed business activity is not executed properly. This is highlighted in the examples related to running payroll and posting a G/L entry.[1] These negative costs or sanctions are associated with either sporadic adverse outcomes resulting from various risks, including the routine and repeated execution (or non-performance) of business activities or from persistently executing the activities ineffectively or sub-optimally.

It is worth noting that the business activities vary greatly in scale but still have the same qualities regarding their financial characteristics. In this sense they are consistent from a financial perspective irrespective of scale and can be analyzed and evaluated similarly. That is, business objectives are intended to yield a positive return, regardless of the scale of the investment or activity.

Proposed Definition of a Control Activity (from a financial perspective)

Using this general definition of business activities, and keeping in mind their financial characteristics outlined above, the investment in a control activity or activities is consistent with that of a standard business activity with one slight variation, as follows:

> *A control is the commitment of scarce resources, (capital, labor and/or materials), required to prevent or mitigate unfavorable outcomes or events (whether intended or not) that have a negative financial return or cost.*

Notice the contrast in the definitions. While business activities are designed to achieve desired (or affirmative) outcomes that have a positive financial return, these activities, through the normal course of execution, can be impacted by or result in unintended undesirable outcomes as well that have a negative financial return. Likewise, other risks that

---

[1]   While they were only called out in the final two examples, these types of unintended costs of poor execution of a business activity or otherwise anomalous outcomes, (e.g., bad luck), could have been assigned to any of the four activities described in **Figure 1.**

are sustained by an entity also result in a negative financial return. Controls are intended to prevent or otherwise mitigate and lessen these undesirable outcomes. In this way, they are both consistent with the definition of a business activity–as controls are business activities too–but achieve the positive return (which is a principal financial characteristic of all organizational activities), in an inverse manner, by reducing a potential negative return. Coming to terms with this definition of control is perhaps the most important underlying concept of this text. For this reason, we will examine it carefully.

Let us, therefore, consider the soundness of the proposed definition in the context of a few examples. The COSO framework divides controls in to five 'internal control' components; Control Environment, Risk Assessment, Control Activities, Information and Communication and Monitoring. While it is not difficult to think of examples of preventive and detective Control Activities whose purpose is to avoid or reduce the impact of adverse outcomes, how this control definition might apply to Information and Communication activities that are a part of an entity's overall control program is less intuitive. Let's consider a couple examples to see if the proposed definition applies well.

Example 1 – A Conflict of Interest Policy (COSO Information and Communication Component)

This would fall under the Information and Communication attribute the COSO framework, as the policy is a method to inform employees of in-force policies and control activities. These policies and control activities would typically include communicating the expectation to the organization's representatives (e.g. employees) that they will not engage in any self-dealing or other conduct that may influence individuals from acting (to the best of their ability) in the best interests of the organization. Obviously an environment where potential conflicts of interest are poorly controlled will lead to a higher likelihood of decision-making and conduct that results in suboptimal economic performance for the organization as individuals may take actions, fraudulently or otherwise, that advance their personal interest ahead of the interest of the organization. In the worst case, an organization that does not have an effective policy and organizational culture that discourages conflicts of interest may suffer significant liabilities or reputational damage. Either way, the outcomes are the same: results for the organization (operational, reputational, or otherwise) are lower than would be achieved if such a policy were in place. While the cost of such an outcome may be hard to quantify, there is no question that the absence of this control results in an expected negative financial outcome.

Example 2 – A Monitoring and Oversight Activity (COSO Monitoring Component)

In terms of a monitoring activity, an illustrative control that is typically present in larger organizations is the practice of preparing a detailed budget forecast of expenses for a fiscal period that management then uses to compare actual expenditures to the budgeted expenditures over the same fiscal period. Clearly we can see that our definition applies well to this situation, as the purpose of the control is to ensure that the various areas that have responsibility for managing a portion of the overall budget do not exceed their approved budget for expenditures unless there is a good reason or special approval is obtained. In this manner, organizations attempt to control or reduce expenditures by discouraging or limiting overages. While this is a poignant example of a monitoring control's central purpose of limiting or avoiding costs, all monitoring controls should operate in a similar fashion. That is, monitoring controls are implemented to identify condition(s) or events that result in unauthorized or unnecessary financial costs in an attempt to avoid or minimize those costs. While there is a broad spectrum of potential monitoring controls we could analyze, most of them fit this profile.

Although simplistic, these definitions are easy to understand and can serve as a viable financial definition of organizational objectives and of controls. That is, the above definitions provide us with the means of applying traditional methods of financial analysis to the investment in controls. For the remainder of this text, we will focus on looking for ways to use these definitions to evaluate investment decisions regarding controls. However, before we outline a suitable approach for the financial analysis of controls, it might be helpful to spend a couple moments gaining an understanding of the many reasons controls have traditionally been excluded or overlooked from the standpoint of financial analysis. Outlining such a list of challenges will help us determine whether or not our proposed framework for the financial analysis of controls has value and is useful in addressing these various challenges.

CHAPTER 3

The Characteristics Of Control From A Financial Standpoint

In my experience, there are many reasons why we neglect to perform an economic evaluation of risk-and-control decisions. Some of these factors include the following:

- **Regulatory Requirements** – Many control requirements are generated by regulatory or legal mandates. For these reasons, organizations view these as requirements in the truest sense, that is, as dictates that *must* be addressed. Because these risk-and-control requirements are perceived to be necessary, many organizations believe that an economic analysis of these controls is not required or beneficial, as there is no decision to make; the costs associated with the requirements will need to be borne by the organization regardless of whether they are evaluated or not.

- **The Costs of Controls Are Not Apparent** – Some organizations consider the costs of implementing controls to be immaterial and/or hard to quantify. The rationale for this view appears to be that many control activities do not require "hard costs" (i.e. additional financial outlays that would not otherwise be incurred), as they can often be performed as additional responsibilities assigned to designated employees without affecting their existing responsibilities. In this sense, these assignments are not perceived to have any additional, quantifiable costs associated with their implementation, and the operation of these controls are deemed to be of minimal cost. If expenses are incurred, they are perceived to be difficult to quantify or "de minimis".

- **Lack of ROI** – As the financial benefit of controls is cost-avoidance, controls are incorrectly deemed to provide no return on investment. As we know from the financial definition of control established earlier, this is not correct. Any cost avoidance realized provides the organization with a positive return, in the sense of a financial cost or cash outflow that was not incurred by the organization that otherwise would have been. However, without a clear or easily identifiable economic benefit, applying standard methods to evaluate controls from an economic standpoint is viewed to be of negligible value for several reasons (a few of which are listed below).

- **Cost of Acquiring Information** – The cost of implementing individual controls is generally modest. For this reason, the cost of acquiring the information needed to perform a financial analysis of the control design, implementation, and operating effectiveness costs is thought to exceed its value in terms of reducing the cost of implementing and operating controls.

- **Informal Decision Making and Implementation Process** – The decision to implement controls is often done on an as-needed, informal basis. As a result, the design and implementation of control is performed in an informal manner without consideration for the cost implications and the expenses incurred.

- **Identifying and Capturing Relevant Costs** -- Although potentially significant, the costs associated with controls are incremental, incurred in a piecemeal fashion, and often implemented in conjunction with other things (for example other process changes or improvements), and the costs associated with the control implementation is hard to isolate and measure.

- **Ancillary and Overlooked** – The costs of controls are generally subordinate to, and minor in scale compared to the overall cost-benefit evaluation associated with most business investment decisions. As such, they are generally not considered or incorporated into the overall business investment decision-making process.

- **Narrow View of Costs** – Control costs are often viewed too narrowly. For example, control costs frequently do not include the ongoing operation, assessment, third-party costs or benefits associated with the control (which may be charged back or passed on to the subject organization). Viewed broadly, controls frequently have primary, secondary, and even tertiary cost implications. Primary costs may be defined as the costs to design, implement, and operate a given control. Secondary costs can be viewed as the costs incurred by the organization to periodically self-assess controls, and tertiary costs would be the costs of third parties assessing an organization's controls, for example external audit costs that are borne by the organization.

- **Psychology and Perspective of the Risk and Control Professional** – The risk-and-control profession tends to attract and advance practitioners who largely disregard cost implications. While that characterization may seem disparaging and outlandish, it is not intended to be. The point is that individuals who excel at this professional discipline need to cultivate a perspective that allows them to be independent and objective and to remain uninfluenced by business objectives and constraints when analyzing risks and evaluating controls. The profession, moreover, calls on the ability to mentally isolate on the risks as well as control design and to evaluate what could go wrong in a theoretical sense, in order to understand risk exposure and/or the flaws in a control design and operation. These skills are different from (and somewhat contrary to) the skills that typically are rewarded in most other roles in an oranization. In general, the profession tends to select and advance those who can dispassionately articulate the risk exposure and potential control flaws in the design and operating effectiveness of a control without bending their analysis and recommendations to the weight of practical considerations and challenges that implementing their recommendations may pose. Typically, the risk-and-control professional leaves the assessment of those implications to others whose task it is to evaluate them (economically or otherwise) by weighing these risk and control considerations and placing them in context with other business priorities and considerations. This is not surprising, as this responsibility is not part of the risk-and-control professional's role.

In summary, there are many understandable reasons why the financial evaluation of controls has been overlooked and underemphasized by the profession and there are several challenges to incorporating financial analysis of risk and control considerations in to an organization's decision-making. In the next chapter, we will explore ways to apply basic financial analysis concepts to some common risk and control decision-making contexts.

CHAPTER 4

A Framework For The Financial Analysis Of Controls

Going back to our definition of control, we defined a control as an activity or set of activities intended to prevent or mitigate certain events that result in adverse financial outcomes. Using this definition, the adverse outcome(s) that a control is intended to eliminate or reduce is another way to describe a risk exposure. An exposure is the description of the adverse outcome(s) that will result from a risk in the absence of controls to reduce its likelihood or severity. It is intended to objectively describe and quantify the adverse outcome that could result in the absence of the given control(s). A quasi-mathematical expression of a (risk) exposure is as follows:

1. **(Risk) Exposure = Adverse Outcome(s) Associated with a Given Risk (or Category or Risks)**

An attempt to translate this negative return or outcome in financial terms would result in the following:

2. **(Risk) Exposure = Cost of the Adverse Outcome(s)**

This expression provides a straightforward starting point to begin our financial analysis of control and to introduce some real-world factors.

To do so, it will be helpful to further refine the definition of an exposure. Specifically, an exposure refers to future unfavorable event(s) of an uncertain probability and size resulting from a given risk (or class of risks). Therefore we have three factors that need to be incorporated into our evaluation of an exposure; an estimate of cost associated with an unfavorable event, its likelihood, and its timing (i.e. an estimate of when [the timeframe and how often] this unfavorable event may occur in the future). I have attempted to express this equation below:

3. **Exposure = Present Value of a Future and Potentially Recurring Unfavorable Event Associated with a Given Risk, or ...**

> the present value of a loss annuity is equal to the estimate of potential loss associated with one instance of the adverse event multiplied by the probability of its occurrence, taking into consideration an estimate of the presumed timing of the adverse event and if this adverse event could happen again, an estimate of the time interval in which it could recur (with the same probability as assigned to the first/next occurrence), and the total number of times the adverse event would recur.

When there is a finite and known number of loss occurrences with a regular frequency/periodicity, the equation for determining the Present Value (or "PV") of an Annuity is as follows:

4. **PV of a (Ordinary) Loss Annuity of N losses = Loss * ((1 - (1 + Annual Discount Factor/T)$^{-N}$) / Annual Discount Factor/T), where....**

PV = present value

Loss = (average) loss per occurrence of risk event

Discount Factor = Interest Rate to reflect the time value of money (e.g. for inflation) as the event will occur in the future

N = Number of loss occurrences.

T = number of times per year (or compounding period) the loss event is expected to occur.

When the loss occurrence is assumed to repeat indefinitely (i.e. an infinite number of loss occurrences), the formula simplifies to the following:

5. PV Loss Annuity (that is perpetual) = Average (Total) Loss (per period)/Discount Factor (per period)

Please note that, for simplicity, these formulas incorporate the following assumptions: that the loss amount and discount factors do not change, the first payment occurs at the end of the period and the risk/loss events occur with regular timing.[2] The above formula reflects the discount factor or the forecasted time value of money, and also factors in the probability of such a loss, if it does occur. In financial analysis, an attempt to quantify a financial return (cost) of an uncertain magnitude and probability is done through the concept of "expected value." This is defined as the sum of all possible outcomes, or rather a summarization of the discrete potential outcomes, multiplied by their estimated probability. Expected value can be represented as follows:

---

2   While these assumptions are inexact forecasted estimates, if the loss events (or payments) are expected to recur many times and the average period of time with which they recur is expected to remain constant over time, this calculated result should be close enough to the true result for the purposes of our analysis. If the amount of each payment is large and the number of payments few, it would be better to estimate the timing of each individual payment and apply a discount factor to each loss payment to arrive at the PV of each loss and to sum the total of those losses to arrive at the overall PV of the series of loss payments.

6. **Loss Exposure = PV (Expected Value [Cost] of Outcome), where Expected Value or EV = Sum of (each discrete outcome * each outcome's probability.)**

The expected value is determined through a process called "Monte Carlo" analysis, whereby all possible discrete outcomes or returns of an event are defined and estimated and then each outcome is assigned a probability of occurring. The probabilities are assigned so that all outcomes are represented, and therefore the probabilities will total 100%, effectively covering the financial return of each potential outcome. Each discrete outcome's probability is then multiplied by the estimated value of the corresponding outcome to determine a weighted amount or return. The weighted returns are summed to determine an overall expected value. While there are a few steps involved, the process is straightforward and intuitive. A simple example has been provided below to help illustrate.

An Example of Expected Value

Assume that there is an exposure to data breach for a large retailer. To determine the expected value/cost of this event, one would attempt to define the potential outcomes as follows:

Outcome 1 – Adverse Outcome Does Not Occur (i.e., a costly data breach never occurs)

You estimate the likelihood of this outcome to be 40%, and the cost, naturally, to be nil, so the expected value would then be $0 for this scenario.

Outcome 2 – Limited Impact Data Breach Occurs (i.e., a breach of modest size and impact occurs)

For this outcome, the organization sustains a limited data breach. Let's suppose that based on historical averages and an assessment of the subject organization's environment, we estimate that the likelihood of this outcome to be 25%. The breach affects just a few users/customers, and the damages, while not trivial, are relatively modest. Nonetheless, the organization estimates that it would sustain approximately $100,000 in additional costs related to the incident, in terms of researching the issue forensically, notifying customers, and providing restitution to users/customers impacted and in terms of the subjective limited cost of damage to the organization's brand and/or reputation.

Outcome 3 – Large Impact Data Breach Occurs (i.e., a breach of major size and impact occurs)

In this scenario, the organization incurs a larger, more widespread and more public data breach. The likelihood of this outcome is also deemed to be 25%. The hard costs incurred in the form of direct damages (for example, similar direct cost categories as outlined in **Outcome 2**, above) and the subjective cost estimate of damage to the organization's brand and reduced future profitability as a result of the loss is estimated to be approximately $1,000,000.

Outcome 4 – Worst Case Scenario (i.e., a devastating breach of the costliest size and impact occurs)

Under the worst case scenario, an organization suffers a major security breach and sustains a huge loss that directly affects a large percentage of the organization's customers. Such an occurrence results in a significant negative impact to an organization's brand and public relations in addition to substantial direct costs in damages, fines and restitution that would also be incurred. The likelihood of this scenario is judged to be 10%, and the cost of such an event is estimated to be approximately $10,000,000.

Given each of the possible scenarios above and applying the using Monte Carlo analysis, the expected value would be as follows:

List of Possible Outcomes	Loss * Probability of Occurrence	Weighted/Expected Value (Loss)
1 – No Data Loss	($0) * 40%	($0)
2 – Limited	($100,000) * 25%	($25,000)
3 – Larger	($1,000,000) * 25%	($250,000)
4 – Worst Case	($10,000,000) * 10%	($1,000,000)
Totals:	100%	($1,275,000)

This analysis would suggest that the expected loss of a data breach event would be $1,275,000, or the sum of each discrete (estimated) loss amount factored by its probability. This analysis can be performed on any event whose magnitude is uncertain. You simply need to approximate the various possible outcomes if the event occurs (or does not) and the negative cash flow or return that will result.

Frequency, Volume, and 'The Time Value of Money'

Now that we have a method to estimate the expected value of a given control risk or potential adverse outcome, we also need to consider the timing and frequency aspects of adverse outcomes in our analysis. To properly value a risk exposure, we need to determine or estimate the number of times the adverse events may occur and their frequency or timing. Given that we cannot predict the amount of a future loss, (the expected value is simply an estimate of its weighted average), it is also impossible to predict the number of times and/or the frequency with which a risk event may occur. Nonetheless, it is important to consider the time horizon under consideration and the nature of the event that you are trying to estimate. For example, we know that, theoretically, a flooding event severe enough to invoke a business continuity program could occur twice in one year. However, for most organizations that are not located in a flood-prone area, this frequency would be highly improbable. Depending upon the climate and location where a facility is situated, it is more likely that such an event will occur infrequently, such as once every twenty-five to fifty years. The point is that in addition to the expected value of a risk event, one also needs to factor in the frequency and timeframe with which such an event may occur.[3]

In keeping with our prior example, we estimate that such a risk event will occur once every fifty years. We also have no way of forecasting with precision at what point during the estimated fifty-year event horizon (or cycle) we are currently situated, unless perhaps, if such an event occurred recently. While it may be possible to refer to the last occurrence of a similar event as the starting point of the once-every-fifty-years cycle, this approach may not be valid for some other potential risk events, as there may not be historical data or events to base the start of the "risk event cycle" upon, depending on the nature of the risk event we are trying to estimate. In this case, it may make sense to assume that, on average, we are at the midpoint between the once-every-fifty-years event. Neither approach is sophisticated or without theoretical flaws and there are certainly other, more exacting methods that can be used to analyze a series of potential future risk events. It is also plausible (or even likely) that, given the dynamic nature of things, the conditions that trigger or affect the likelihood and frequency of the loss event will change over time, a fact that may impact the likelihood, frequency, or severity of the loss event over time. While it is possible to factor and build this information into the financial analysis to make it more robust and precise, generally the ability to forecast and incorporate such nuances into the analysis is difficult, making them impractical or non-cost-effective. Therefore, for the range of most risk-and-control financial analyses and decision-making, the less sophisticated methods are typically sufficient, as the time and effort needed to use a more sophisticated method of valuation will likely exceed the value derived in terms of greater precision and better decision-making. Use of more sophisticated models would, furthermore, suggest a degree of accuracy in the estimation process that does

---

3   Doing this is especially important for infrequent events with large loss amounts.

not exist, implying a false sense of precision to the analysis. For this reason, in the absence of other information regarding the likely timing of the once-every-fifty-years event, we would assume that such an event would occur approximately twenty-five years in the future, which would then be the length of time for discounting the future cost of the negative cash flow back to the present. You would then apply a Present Value Factor (or PVF) for twenty-five years using the best estimate of the discount rate/factor to determine an estimate [in today's dollars] of the potential cost avoidance that could be realized by the implementation of a business continuity plan. This information could then be used by an organization to determine the maximum amount of investment it is willing to commit to developing a business continuity program. This analysis may reveal trade-off opportunities to maximize the return on the investment in a business continuity plan through realizing the "80-20" rule--that is the idea that it may be possible to realize 80% of the benefit of a desired outcome with only 20% of the effort or cost--by analyzing the reduction in the severity of the future loss event that occurs with varying levels of investment in a business continuity plan/capability and choosing the one that has the best "net present value" (or "NPV"), which takes into consideration the combination of the residual loss sustained and the cost invested in the mitigating control, in this case, a business continuity program. Such an analysis generally promotes an approach whereby the investment in the control may be less than originally planned, as the NPV of the combined cost of the control implementation and the residual expected loss is the least.

Therefore, to summarize, this chapter went over basic methods and considerations for quantifying a risk exposure, factoring in the nature, probability and timing of risk events. In addition, a method to quantify future loss events and to discount them using present value factors into today's 'dollars' was also explored. In the next chapter, we will examine how these financial analysis factors should be applied and how they can drive decision making.

CHAPTER 5

Practical Implications Of A Financial Analysis Of Control

Now that we outlined a rudimentary method to estimate the losses that may occur from a given risk area, how can this information be used to render better decisions from a financial standpoint regarding the investment in the design, implementation, and operation of controls? What general relationships and guidelines exist that would help organizations implement a more financially efficient and effective control environment? Admittedly it is hard to quantify the cost impact of one control or several controls, or even for a large project to address control risks, for that matter. However, there are features of control design and operation which may magnify or minimize these costs. By considering these factors it is hoped that an organization can choose more cost-efficient controls, or at least design and operate controls more efficiently. Some of these characteristics include the following:

- Complexity – Controls with more complex design or that require a high degree of professional judgment are harder to operate and assess.
- Design attributes – The type of control implemented and its design features may drive its costs. For example, once configured

(i.e. designed and implemented), automated controls are generally less expensive to operate and easier to monitor and assess than controls that require a higher degree of human execution and judgment.

- Diligence and Judgment – Controls that require a high degree of diligence or professional judgment are generally more expensive to operate and may have a lower effectiveness, due to human fallibility.

- Auditability of the control – The relative ease (or difficulty) with which the design, implementation, and operating effectiveness of a control can be evaluated and evidenced can impact a control's cost.

- Reports - Controls whose execution or assessment require the use of reports or other artifacts that require validation of their completeness and accuracy (for example, if they have a role in internal control over financial reporting, or ICFR) will impact costs.

Based on the aspects listed above and what has been presented earlier, some basic methods and factors to consider to effect a cost-effective control environment are listed below.

- Consider secondary costs (and if applicable, tertiary costs) of controls in addition to the primary control-execution costs.

- Automated controls, once operational, are generally more efficient and effective than controls that require manual execution.

- While redundant controls (or a "defense-in-depth") approach may be necessary to mitigate a risk effectively, depending on the residual risk, the controls will provide diminishing returns on investment and therefore may become non-economic. If taken to an extreme, they will provide negligible benefits.

- Similar to the redundancy described above, overachievement of a control objective (i.e. effectively eliminating a risk exposure) may not be justifiable from a financial perspective.

- "Tone-at-the-Top" Controls and other components of Internal Control are the hardest to quantify in terms of their costs and benefits from a financial perspective. On the other hand, these activities often do not carry significant hard (out-of-pocket) costs and therefore may be cost-effective in their overall effect on an organization's control environment.

- While generally considered necessary, regulatory edicts nonetheless have unique cost/benefit considerations that should be evaluated carefully from a financial standpoint.

- Mixed control/operational activities need to be evaluated both from a control (avoiding an adverse outcome and its related cost) and a positive business objective standpoint (promoting the achievement of a desired operational outcome, which results in additional revenue and/or reduced costs). Failure to consider both aspects of these mixed activities may undervalue the financial benefits of implementing the control.

- Reducing the control burden through a periodic process of evaluating the control environment and revising controls by rationalizing them. In this section, we go over an important feature of implementing and maintaining an effective and efficient control environment, which is a process to periodically review the control estate to look for opportunities to reduce the control burden by eliminating and revising controls. This process is described last as it is a critical, complementary process that should apply the methods described in this text to correct the natural tendency for the control estate to become over-engineered and complex over time.

Each of the factors outlined above are examined briefly below.

Considering Secondary (Non-Direct) Costs Associated with Controls

When considering the costs of the design and operation of a control, it is important to understand the non-direct costs of controls in addition to the direct costs. Costs could include payroll[4] associated with employee time as well as other variable costs that would not otherwise have been incurred without the implementation of the control(s). A broad categorization of these costs is listed below.

Category	Description	Examples
Primary (or Direct) Costs	Costs incurred directly in the design, implementation, and operation of a control. (Borne by the entity.)	Cost of control design, software purchase, configuration, testing, implementation, control execution, reconciliation, etc.

---

4   Please note that payroll costs are generally considered fixed in the near term, and therefore consideration should be given to whether and how much payroll cost is incurred in the design, implementation and operation of controls. The point is that if an employee is utilized less than 100% currently and his or her payroll is a fixed cost, there may be no additional (direct) cost incurred with the expenditure of the employee's time in connection with the design, implementation, and operation of a control. For the purpose of this analysis, we will assume that all employees are fully utilized and taking on the additional responsibility of designing, implementing, and/ or operating a control involves a direct cost, or at least an opportunity cost. That is, if an employee's time was not expended in connection with a given control, his or her time and payroll could be spent working on something else of equal or greater value. In this sense, the cost of employee's time ("fully-loaded" payroll rate) should be considered a direct cost of the enterprise attributable to having added the control to the control environment. This assumption is generally appropriate for most financial analyses for decision-making and, if applied consistently to business decisions, should result in an accurate assignment of costs to the control.

Category	Description	Examples
Secondary Costs	Costs to monitor and assess the design, implementation, and operating effectiveness of a control. (Generally borne by the entity.)	Management testing of controls, monitoring of controls, review of dashboards on which control execution is reported, reporting on the results of management's controls. Time spent by management in the remediation in response to noted control deficiency, etc. This category can be thought of as the overhead associated with "owning" controls.
Tertiary Costs	Costs for third parties to obtain control assurance and monitor controls. (Borne by third parties, but increased costs may be charged back to the entity.)	External auditor costs associated with evaluating the control design and operating effectiveness, effort spent providing information to client organization regarding the control. Effort and resources expended in providing control assurance to regulatory authorities regarding the control. This category includes costs that may be incurred by other third-party entities as a result of the controls an organization implements. Sometimes these costs are charged back to the organization, and in other cases, they are sustained by the third party entities.

Advantages of Automated Controls

Automated controls have several features that can lower their cost. These features are well understood by most risk and control professionals and are intuitive. They include the following:

- Configuration – Generally automated controls require only a one-time configuration. Once set up, they rarely need to be changed, and generally the ongoing cost of administrating the control is negligible. Non-automated controls may require set-up (configuration) with each execution. Sometimes this setup can be expensive from a resource or time perspective.
- Automated – the performance is automated and does not rely on human execution. The performance of the control, therefore, is generally consistent and error-free (and requires no effort, per se, only CPU cycles.)
- System Enforced – Similarly, because the control is automated, it is invoked and enforced consistently. Circumventing an automated control is more difficult.
- Testing – Because the human element is eliminated, the testing of the control is a straightforward matter of obtaining system evidence of its design and operating effectiveness. This evidence is often recorded on the system and easily accessed, (i.e., a screen print illustrating execution of the control is often sufficient.)

As you can see, automated controls enjoy several advantages from a cost standpoint.

Cost Implications of a Defense-In-Depth Strategy

A popular and time-tested approach in the risk-and-control profession is to implement several overlapping or duplicative controls to address a risk exposure, invoking what is termed a "defense-in-depth" strategy. The rationale for this strategy is that if you implement just one control, that control may not reduce the risk exposure to an acceptably low level, so additional controls are implemented to obtain the desired degree of reduction in the residual risk exposure. This process may be repeated several times, sometimes to the point where the risk exposure is effectively eliminated. The issue with this approach is that if you assume each of the defense-in-depth controls is roughly the same cost, the cost associated with addressing the risk doubles and triples with the implementation of each additional control after the first. However, the financial benefit in terms of reducing the risk exposure generally diminishes significantly with the addition of each successive control. This method is sometimes repeated to the point where the financial benefit associated with implementing the control in terms of a reduction in the related risk exposure is negligible and the cost associated with each control remains roughly equal.[5]

The following example provides an illustration of this principle:

Example

Let's assume that an organization has a risk exposure to unauthorized physical access to a sensitive company facility to which they have assigned an expected value (cost) of ($5,000,000) over a specified period, which we will assume to be twenty years[6]. (Please note that for simplicity we have disregarded the time value of money in this example.) To address this risk, it has opted to implement a defense-in-depth strategy as follows:

---

5   For purposes of illustration, the cost of each defense-in-depth control implemented was assumed to be equal, when in fact the cost of these controls could vary widely. The point is that with a defense-in-depth strategy, the financial benefit derived from the reduction in the risk will diminish significantly with each additional control that is implemented, whereas the cost of each control is generally independent of the other controls implemented and has no relationship to, and is frequently not evaluated in relation to, the scale of the residual risk.

6   For this example, a twenty-year time horizon was chosen to value both the risk exposure and the associated control costs. This was done for two reasons. First, it was done in an effort to equate the period of the control costs to a commensurate period of the risk exposure, which is required for proper analysis, and secondly, because this was deemed to be the longest time horizon for which the assumptions regarding the (a) valuation of risk exposure and (b) the operating costs of the associated controls could be reasonably projected. Admittedly the choice of this time period and the associated costs were highly subjective and used for the purpose of this example only.

#	Control Description	Control Cost	Risk Reduction	Value of Reduction
1	Implement a card key access system to the restricted facility	$200,000@yr for 20 years Total Cost = $4,000,000	Control reduces the likelihood of (and the resulting expected value of costs associated with) unauthorized access by 80%	$4,000,000 ($5,000,000 * 80%) Residual Exposure = $1,000,000
2	Hire a security guard to monitor the facility	$50,000@yr for 20 years Total Cost = $1,000,000	Control reduces the likelihood of (and the resulting expected value of residual costs associated with) unauthorized access by 80%.	$800,000 ($1,000,000 * 80%) Residual Exposure = $200,000
3	Install cameras with 24-hour monitoring of facility	$7,500@yr for 20 years Total Cost = $150,000	Control reduces the likelihood of (and the resulting expected value of residual costs associated with) unauthorized access by 80%.	$160,000 ($200,000 * 80%) Residual Exposure = $40,000
4	Hire a security service to monitor the facility with automatic silent alarm and guaranteed response within four minutes of alarm	$5,000@yr for 20 years Total Cost = $100,000	Control reduces the likelihood of (and the resulting expected value of residual costs associated with) unauthorized access by 80%.	$32,000 ($40,000 * 80%) Residual Exposure = $8,000

While it may seem improbable that an organization would implement all four of these controls, I have seen organizations that have implemented a similar set of overlapping physical security controls. As you can see, this approach is doubly poor from an economic standpoint. First, the total cost of controls implemented and operated over the time period ($5,250,000) exceeds the overall risk exposure ($5,000,000) it is intended to address. Secondly, while each control is equally effective at reducing the residual risk (by 80%), because of the dramatic reduction in the residual risk that results from implementing several controls to address the same risk exposure the cost of two of the four controls implemented (2 and 4 above) is greater than the residual risk exposure it addresses (with the cost of control 4 being much higher than the remaining residual risk). While the example chosen may not be typical in many respects–for example each control was defined as being equally effective at addressing the risk (i.e. each control resulted in the same 80% residual risk reduction)—the example does illustrate a common characteristic of a defense-in-depth control strategy, which is the financial benefit derived from implementing additional controls diminishes rapidly with a defense-in-depth strategy, while the cost of those additional controls may not..[7]

The Cost of Risk Elimination: Balancing Control Cost with the Value of Reducing Risk

Similar to the point noted above, organizations and risk-and-control professionals are often confronted with options for alternative controls or control design to address a given risk exposure. In most cases, when choosing between alternatives, the organization will opt for the control that is most effective at eliminating the risk exposure, provided the costs and cost differential of the alternatives are not prohibitive. That is, organizations will generally choose the control that will reduce the risk exposure to the lowest level, irrespective of the difference in costs. If the cost differential between the controls is not great, this

---

7   The cost of each control may, in fact, increase if more sophisticated methods and attributes are required in the design and operation of each additional control in order to eliminate the remaining residual risk.

choice is generally the correct one. However, when the cost of the control alternatives varies greatly and the difference in the reduction of risk exposure is modest, choosing the most "effective" control may not be the best choice from a financial standpoint.

To illustrate this point, we will go back to our physical security example and consider the following scenarios.

Background: As described in **III,** above, the organization has a facility that needs to be protected against unauthorized physical access. Assume a similar fact pattern as outlined above for the value of risk exposure, although the costs and the effectiveness of the controls have been adjusted for the purpose of this illustration. Consider the following scenarios and alternatives:

Scenario A – Two Alternatives, Different Costs, Most Effective Control is the Most Cost-Efficient

#	Control Description	Control Cost	Risk Reduction	Value of Reduction
A	Implement a card key access system to the restricted facility	$500,000 over 20 years	Control reduces the likelihood (and the resulting expected value of costs associated with) unauthorized access by 99%	PV of $4,950,000 ($5,000,000 * 99%) NPV of $4,450,000 = (Risk Reduction – Cost) OR ($4,950,000 - $500,000)
B	Install cameras with 24-hour monitoring of facility	$350,000 over 20 years	Control reduces the likelihood (and the resulting expected value of costs associated with) unauthorized access by 80%	PV of $4,000,000 ($5,000,000 * 80%) NPV of $3,650,000 = ($4,000,000 - $350,000)

Scenario B – Two Alternatives, Different Costs, Most Effective Control is NOT the Most Cost-Efficient

#	Control Description	Control Cost	Risk Reduction	Value of Reduction
A	Implement a card key access system to the restricted facility	$500,000 over 20 years	Control reduces the likelihood (and the resulting expected value of costs associated with) unauthorized access by 99%	PV of reduction in exposure = $4,950,000 ($5,000,000 * 99%) NPV of $4,450,000 = ($4,950,000 - $500,000)
B	Assign keys to authorized personnel. Monitor the activity and entry into the facility via a camera surveillance. Manually administrate and track the assignment of keys to personnel	$100,000 over 20 years	Control reduces the likelihood (and the resulting expected value of costs associated with) unauthorized access by 95%	PV of reduction in exposure = $4,750,000 ($5,000,000 * 95%) NPV of $4,650,000 = ($4,750,000 - $100,000)

In **Scenario A**, the control that yields the greatest reduction in the risk exposure is also the most cost-efficient. However, in **Scenario B**, the control that is less effective in reducing the risk exposure is, nonetheless, the most cost-efficient alternative. This illustrates that controls should not be chosen solely on the basis of their effectiveness in reducing risk exposure, or by choosing the solution that yields the lowest residual exposure, but, rather, in terms of their *overall* financial assessment, which factors in the effectiveness (in terms of reducing the risk exposure) *and* cost of the control.

The Financial Analysis of Controls with 'Soft' or 'Control Environment Overhead' Costs.

A strong control environment depends on implementing the various components of internal control. In fact, the <u>COSO 2013 Internal Control–Integrated Framework</u> (*Committee of Sponsoring Organizations of the Treadway Commission, 2013*) identifies five components, as follows:

- Control Environment
- Risk Assessment
- Control Activities
- Information and Communication
- Monitoring

Of these components, in the view of the author, only one ties directly to the reduction of a risk exposure, and that is the Control Activities component. The rest of the component areas, although deemed necessary to effect a sound internal control environment, typically have an indirect, yet pervasive and hard-to-measure effect on reducing a specific risk exposure. As a result it is easier (although not easy, per se) to isolate and quantify the costs attributable to the design, implementation, and operation of control activities and the resulting reduction in risk exposure(s) from a financial standpoint than it is for the activities of the other COSO components of Internal Control. That is, the other components of Internal Control either support the deployment of controls to reduce risks (Control Activities) or promote a good culture that benefits an organization's control environment by generally reducing the probability of a wide spectrum of risk exposures by promoting diligence, quality, and ethical behavior in an organization. However, from the standpoint of this analysis, these additional activities and components, which in many cases aim to improve the organization's control culture or Tone-At-The-Top, are often harder to analyze from a financial standpoint. These components, furthermore, frequently involve soft costs, such as payroll, as opposed to hard costs which would not otherwise be incurred. As we discussed earlier, soft costs are harder to quantify and are somewhat fixed in the near term. Therefore, they present the challenges of being difficult to quantify and allocate to a control activity and may not, therefore, have a bearing on the decision from an opportunity cost perspective which limits consideration in economic decision making to costs that vary based on the decision alternatives under consideration. Both of these factors add to the difficulty of incorporating these components and their associated financial costs and benefits into a financial analysis. When evaluating the value of these control components, we also need to consider that, when it comes to these complementary components of control, the sum, (when the components are combined in the right measure), is generally greater than its parts. That is, evaluating each of these factors individually from a financial perspective will yield a total benefit that is less than the components combined, given their synergism in improving control. Therefore, determining the relative benefits of each component used alone and in combination (and in which amounts, to use a cooking metaphor) is difficult and a matter of professional judgment. Simply stated, determining the correct combination of these internal control components is more a matter of judgment and experience, in my view, than it is a subject that lends itself to traditional financial analysis. In summary, the advice to the practitioner, when considering these other, softer components of control from a financial perspective is to recognize and understand the complementary nature of these components along with the point that their inclusion is advisable or necessary to have an effective control process and environment and to design the suite of control components and measures needed to address a given risk exposure accordingly.

For the reasons listed above, it is important to consider the synergism of the control components in our financial analysis. To do so consider the approaches outlined below.

- When analyzing control activities for financial analysis, consider their linkage to these other internal control components and attempt to allocate some costs to the control analysis for these other aspects of the control. For example, you may want to allocate some overhead costs to the analysis of the control to reflect the Risk Assessment, Information and Communication, and Monitoring costs that are required to properly design, implement, and operate a related control, or

- Exclude these costs and focus on the opportunity costs associated with the control alternatives. This approach endorses focusing only on the costs of control alternatives that vary based on the decision and requires an objective view of the quantifiable impact the control will have on reducing the risk exposure. In other words, this approach focuses only on a realistic estimate of the costs associated with the control and the reduction in risk exposure that will result.

If the excluded costs will be incurred irrespective of the decision to implement a control or not, this approach is preferable from a pure financial analysis decision-making standpoint. While we have outlined two alternative approaches to these Internal Control components above, either method is defendable and should inform the practitioner's decision-making appropriately, provided the method is consistently applied. In terms of the Tone-At-The-Top activities, these efforts generally affect an organization's culture and behavior and are, therefore, hard to evaluate from a financial standpoint. Let's take training programs, for example, such as a sexual harassment or security awareness training. In both cases, it is hard to quantify the baseline risk exposure an organization has to sexual harassment claims or security-breach incidents and their associated costs. Likewise, it is even more difficult to determine the impact of the training on reducing the risk exposure. However, it does not mean that these "softer" internal control components and activities cannot benefit from financial analysis. In many cases, these programs do not carry significant "hard" (out-of-pocket) costs and therefore the training program may be cost-effective in its overall effect on an organization's control environment, if it results in a significant reduction in risk exposure. In other cases, the cost of the training is easier to determine (for example, if an outside training service is contracted), but the risk that is being addressed is outsized. Let's assume, for example, the cost of developing and administering the training is $25,000 and the risk exposure is, for example, 100 times larger ($2,500,000.) In such a case, the investment in training can be justified if the training results in (at least) a very minor reduction in the risk exposure (i.e., greater than 1%). These efforts, moreover, may have benefits beyond the reduction in exposure of a certain risk or class of risks, in terms of improving organizational culture and conduct that should also be considered. This concept in financial analysis is explored in VII, below. In summary, training and other communication processes and controls often involve fewer hard costs and may also have a broad range of benefits, such as promoting improved results operationally, that need to be considered in evaluating them from a financial standpoint.

Considerations for the Financial Analysis of Regulatory Guidance

As alluded to earlier, regulatory guidance presents a unique set of challenges from a financial analysis point of view. As they are generally required, the decision at hand is not *whether* but, rather, *how* an organization will choose to address a regulatory authority's edicts. Furthermore, as much of the regulatory guidance is prescriptive in nature (i.e. outlining in detail what an organization is expected to do to address regulatory concerns), organizations may have little freedom as to how they address the requirement. The regulatory guidance, furthermore, may not address a specific risk to the organization, but rather may target objectives and risks that lie outside an individual entity's reward matrix. That is, they may promote societal objectives (e.g. clean environment, consumer protection, or systemic risks to the economy) rather than aims that benefit the subject organization.

Therefore, the traditional approach to the financial analysis of control espoused in this book—that is, estimating a risk exposure to the entity and measuring the reduction in the risk exposure that results from the implementation of controls—needs to be modified, as we are not necessarily addressing a risk exposure to the organization, but rather a regulatory edict. Moreover, because these requirements are generally viewed as mandatory, most organizations presume that performing an analysis of the associated costs and potential benefits of controls to address these requirements is moot. These challenges aside, in the case of regulatory requirements, the benefits of determining alternatives to address the requirements and evaluating alternatives from a financial standpoint can be significant. For this reason, it is one of the most important topics of this text, in my estimation.

First, and to place these requirements in proper perspective, it is worth spending a few moments exploring whether the regulatory requirements are truly mandatory. One could argue with good reason that even "mandatory" requirements may be optional in the sense that an organization may want to consider the financial cost-benefit of not complying. While this approach is generally not advisable for many reasons, such as maintaining the organization's brand image and positive image as an ethical and law-abiding organization, it may, nonetheless, be useful to estimate the risk exposure of noncompliance as an alternative, even if the organization has every intention of fully complying. If for no other reason than to present a straw-man alternative to compare with other alternatives that may be available, doing so will help inform the financial analysis and decision, especially if the cost implications of complying with the regulation are cost prohibitive[8].

---

8   In addition, analysis may be helpful in establishing the costs of compliance associated with severe or impractical regulations as compared to the cost of noncompliance. Doing so, for example, may be helpful in influencing the regulatory authority or working with the authority to find other less cost-prohibitive means to satisfy regulatory aims. Likewise, outlining the noncompliance alternative may provide a basis for lobbying the regulatory authority to relax or revise regulations so they are not as onerous and/or impractical to implement or, potentially, to encourage the postponement of their implementation.

As outlined above, we need to adjust the financial analysis framework for analyzing regulatory requirements. Therefore, to properly evaluate the risk of noncompliance (a) the likely cost of fines and other sanctions that could be assessed, (b) the probability of enforcement of those fines and sanctions over a specified period, and (c) any other traditional risk exposures that the implementation of the regulatory guidance may reduce, needs to be estimated. Other than factoring an estimate of these compliance costs into the overall estimate of the risk exposure, the approach and analysis employed is the same as previously outlined. As in all cases, the method used to evaluate alternatives to addressing a regulatory edict will vary depending on the situation and context. One recommended approach is to estimate and assess three general alternatives; noncompliance, full compliance or a combination of the two - partial compliance. The noncompliance and full compliance options are described below.

Option A – Noncompliance (NC): Estimate the expected value (i.e. the fines and other sanctions and the probability of their assessment) of not acting upon the regulatory edict. Ensure that a broad view of the risk exposure is taken that includes other costs, such as the potentially large negative impact the organization could sustain to its brand image or the potential legal costs that could result from noncompliance. Apply the framework described earlier, including a Monte Carlo analysis of the probability of various possible outcomes. The cost-benefit of this option is simply the PV of this total combined risk exposure, which is formulated as follows:

NC Cost-Benefit = PV of Potential Fines and Sanction Costs * Probability of Detection * Probability of Assessment * The Assessment Factor + PV of Traditional Risk Exposure [if applicable] + PV of Other Costs (Harm to Brand Image and Goodwill from not complying, Potential Legal Fees, etc. [if applicable.]

In the above formula, the probability of detection is the likelihood that noncompliance with the regulation will be detected and probability of enforcement is the likelihood that, if detected, the noncompliance will be assessed fines and sanctions, and the assessment factor reflects the percentage of the potential fines and sanctions outlined in the regulatory statute that is actually levied. As you can see, these three factors represent a joint probability, meaning that all three factors need to be incurred (multiplied together) to have the negative outcome realized, such as a fine or sanction being assessed, which (as will be demonstrated) can significantly reduce the expected value of the total regulatory (or risk) exposure. This is an important point to consider with regulatory mandates. For example, if you assume that the potential fines for noncompliance are $100,000, the likelihood of detection 85% (high probability) and the likelihood of assessment is 80% (high probability) and the assessment to be 50% (a significant assessment factor) of the maximum fine, then the expected value (or the total regulatory exposure) associated with the noncompliance with the regulation is below.

$100,000 * (.85 [detection] *.8 [likelihood of assessment] * .5 [percentage of total assessable fine]) = $34,000

It is clear from this example that after factoring in realistic assumptions regarding the detection, assessment, and likely amount of fines and sanctions associated with noncompliance with regulation(s), the potential fine of $100,000 drops down significantly to $34,000, with a combined or joint probability cost factor of just 34%. While this combined probability factor for the detection, assessment, and fine amount seems low, it might actually be high, depending on the circumstances. In fact, many regulatory authorities would be pleased if they were able to detect 85% of all noncompliance instances, fine 80% of those they detect and then assess on average a fine that is 50% of the maximum permitted by the statute. The point of the example is that while the regulation and fines may seem severe, once you adjust for these factors, the amount of a probable sanction will generally be reduced substantially, making noncompliance—at least from a financial standpoint—a more viable option than it is generally considered to be. There is also the time factor of money to consider, if there is a long lag between detection, assessment, and the timeframe provided for payment of the ultimate fine. In fact, if a lengthy litigation or appeal process is involved, the time frame could be several years. If so, it could result in a further significant reduction in the expected value of the eventual fine for noncompliance.

Option B – Full Compliance (FC): In this option, you will use the total risk exposure estimated above as the risk exposure and add to it the additional cost of designing, implementing and operating the control to address the regulatory requirement and subtract from it the benefit of reducing or eliminating the noncompliance risk exposure and the reduction in the (related) traditional risk exposure(s), if any. This approach is formulated as follows:

> **FC Cost-Benefit = NC Cost-Benefit (i.e., total (loss) amount calculated above) + Reduction in costs (both NC cost and reduction in traditional risk exposures) that results from compliance - the costs associated with the design, implementation, and operation of the compliance remedies and related controls.**

The costs of compliance are estimated using the same approach described earlier in the text.

Considering Operational as well as Risk/Control Benefits

One of the concepts we have touched upon that merits closer examination is the importance of considering other benefits that may be realized with the implementation of controls. A good example would be the costs and benefits associated with the implementation of a vendor management program. Typically the impetus and primary cost driver of this effort may be the reduction in control-related risk exposures associated with vendor risk management. For example, when evaluating these programs from a financial standpoint, we will primarily focus on the control-related benefits, such as the benefit of closely vetting a potential business partner or establishing standard reporting protocols to monitor these business partners from a control standpoint, etc. However, the implementation of these risk management programs may also yield a wide range of operational, profit, and cost-benefit that extends beyond the value that is realized from a strictly risk-reduction standpoint. For example, economic benefits may accrue from the implementation of service level agreements that often accompany the implementation of a vendor management program or from the opportunity to negotiate for better fees and services that may be realized as part of an enhanced vendor evaluation process. In general, a robust vendor management program that is frequently implemented along with the specified controls needed to address regulatory requirements may have significant financial implications for overall services levels, cost reduction, and profitability. These benefits should also be factored into the financial analysis of controls as well as the reduction in risk exposure that may be the primary reason for their implementation.

Periodic Control Rationalization – A Critical Process for Maintaining Cost-Effectiveness and Simplicity

In the previous sections we have outlined many considerations to take into account from a financial standpoint. The hope and expectation is that, if these considerations are applied correctly and consistently, the resulting control environment will be both cost-effective and sound from the standpoint of effecting a control environment that is effective in addressing, efficiently, the many risk (and regulatory) exposures facing the entity. In short, the consistent application of the considerations and principles outlined in this work should, theoretically, yield a control environment that has a roster of controls that has been optimized, vis-à-vis alternatives, from a financial effectiveness standpoint. That is, the entity's overall control environment should reflect an ongoing and repetitive process by which identified risk exposures are catalogued, valued, and mitigated in a cost-efficient manner.

The analysis process ensures that the most cost-effective control is designed and implemented when compared to identified alternatives. Therefore, the recommended financial analysis process should contribute to a control environment that is increasingly efficient and effective. Nonetheless, it is important for organizations to assess, periodically, the overall control environment, looking for opportunities to eliminate or to rationalize controls in order to optimize the control environment. Such a periodic review process is recommended, because there is a natural tendency to drift toward an increasingly complex control environment over time. If unchecked, this natural drift may result in an unwieldy and over-engineered "control estate" that will result in a sub-optimal and less-efficient control environment.

Why does this happen? Typically the control estate grows large and complex because the revision process and recommendations described in this text will, over time, result in the continuous introduction of new or revised controls as new or revised risks are identified. However, the process of implementing new and revised controls may not account for the effect they can have on the existing processes and controls or identify the opportunities to eliminate or revise existing controls as a result of the implementation of new controls, for example due to some overlap, redundancy or impairment (related to adverse interaction) among controls.

In addition, the process we have outlined is optimal (compared to designated control alternatives) as of a point in time (the time of the financial assessment of the control alternatives) and assumes that both the operating costs of the control and the expected value (and nature) of the risk exposure it is intended to address are static, which is unrealistic. If any of these attributes change materially over time the corresponding control(s) implemented may no longer be optimal. This situation tends to occur even if you apply the methods outlined earlier in this text in a disciplined manner. Therefore, the ongoing design and implementation of new and revised controls, if unchecked, may result in an overdone and bloated control environment or one that is no longer optimal in relation the underlying risk exposures the control estate was implemented to address, due to changes in those corresponding risk exposures or the design or operating cost-effectiveness of the overall control estate since the time the controls were implemented. For this reason, it is important to periodically review an organization's control estate to look for opportunities to eliminate or rationalize controls throughout the environment, in order to compensate for these factors.

This aspect of implementing a financially efficient control environment is addressed last in this work, because it is perhaps the most important factor in *maintaining* an optimized control environment, as it will serve to correct and reverse the natural tendency to implement too many controls and to acquire an overly complex control estate, or to operate controls whose design or operating costs are no longer cost-effective due to changes in their cost-effectiveness or the corresponding risk exposure, over time, even if all of the previous recommendations in this text are applied well. As such, implementing a robust periodic process to rationalize the control environment is an indispensable feature of an organization's goal to implement a financially efficient and effective control environment.

Rationalization Opportunities

Opportunities to rationalize controls abound in most organizations. There are three broad components of control execution–process, people, and technology. Examining each of these areas can reveal a broad range of opportunities to rationalize or improve the efficiency of controls. Some examples include the following:

Process Opportunities

This is the area on which risk-and-control professionals primarily focus—identifying controls and processes that are in place and evaluating their design and their interaction with other controls and processes. Some examples of the rationalization opportunities include the following:

Opportunity A – Belt-and-Suspenders Redundancies – These are the low-hanging fruit of the rationalization process, redundant controls that address the same risk or perform the same function. As described earlier, redundancy is often needed to effect a cost-effective defense-in-depth approach. Depending on the circumstances, however, it may be more cost-effective to remove one or more of the redundant controls. A hypothetical example of such a control might be the following:

> **Insurance Claim Check Issuance Control(s):** Prior to advances in claims disbursement automation, an insurance company implemented a policy requiring two manual signatures on checks above a certain threshold ($5,000) prior to disbursement. The signatures included one by the claims representative and another by the branch claims manager. However, the system that generates the check has automated functionality that requires a dual authorization by the claims representative and the branch claims manager prior to printing. If an assessment of the design and operation of the system (including the check printing, check stock security features, electronic signature and disbursement process) demonstrates that the system is effective in authenticating the approvers and requiring the dual online approval, one may conclude that the control requiring dual manual signatures on the check is redundant and that manual control can be eliminated.

Opportunity B – Redesigning an Existing Control — Redesigning an existing control typically takes two forms. In the first case, a control is expanded to justify eliminating another control (or controls). In the second method, a control is redesigned to reduce the cost of operating the control.

A more detailed example of these two forms of redesigning an existing control is outlined in the following scenario:

Healthcare Worker Background Checks: Every year a hospital hires many workers for various roles. With the increasing liability placed on health organizations to hire ethical and qualified workers, the health care system commissions a background check for all new hires and un-vetted contractors. After hiring or contracting, the hospital goes through an additional process of commissioning drug testing for all new hires and verifying licensing for credentialed physicians and nurses (only). Each of these processes—drug testing and license verification—costs $100. However, the service that provides the background check will, for an additional $25, verify the licensing for new hires that require it, and drug test each new hire for an additional $75. If you assume the hospital hires a one hundred people a year and only 50% require license verification, the annual cost breaks down as follows:

Services	Current Control Process	Cost	Proposed Control Process	Cost
Drug Test costs	100 People times $100	$10,000	100 people times $75	$7,500
License Verification	50 People times $100	$5,000	50 people times $25	$1,250
		Totals:	**$15,000**		**$8,750**

As you can see in this hypothetical example, adding these two control attributes—drug testing for all hires and license verification for licensed hires—to an existing control process (pre-hire background verification), the organization will reduce annual costs for drug tests and license verification by approximately 42%, [9] as well as eliminating an existing control, as mentioned above.

Opportunity C – Redesigning (Simplifying) an Existing Control – In some cases an existing control can be redesigned (rather than eliminated) to improve the cost efficiency of controls. To illustrate this principle, we will look at data backup and recovery controls, an area that is often rife with opportunities to reduce costs through redesign and simplification of existing controls. Consider the following scenario:

> **Data Backup Procedures:** Many data backup and recovery procedures were designed and implemented long ago, before the revolution in technology that has brought virtualization, vastly increased network capacity and speed, and the ability to mirror production data easily and inexpensively to a private or public cloud in real time. In addition, many organizations' backup procedures still use removable backup media such as tape or offline memory disk. Furthermore, the backup strategy—defining what needs to be backed up and the frequency of backup–may have been defined when critical application processing was still done in batch and discrete cycles—i.e. daily, weekly, monthly, quarterly, and/or annual cycles—adding further cost and complexity to the process. Considering this point and the fact that most large IT organizations have highly redundant, mirrored production environments with "hot failover" capability, reduces the reliance on tape backups. As a result there may be an opportunity to eliminate the extent to which online data is backed up to offline physical media, or at least reduce the frequency and amount of data that needs

---

9   Keep in mind that in this illustrative example, the reduction represents only the hard savings (reduction in direct cash expenses) that may result from the control redesign. The savings does not reflect the reduction in potential liability that may result from replacing a control that results in dismissing a recently hired employee (when you perform license verification after hiring) with a process that confirms this before hiring.

to be stored offline. If the intention is to back up this data to restore it at a disaster-recovery "hot-site," in some cases this arrangement is obsolete, as the entire production environment is mirrored to a geographically remote data center, and processing can be activated instantaneously through a "failover" feature to the other processing site, as needed.

As you can see from the scenario above, many organizations could benefit from evaluating and, if indicated, revamping their backup process, such as curtailing the extent to which offline backup media is created, as the existing arrangement may need to be updated, given technology advances. This change could result in significant cost savings. The control activity is considered redesigned as backing up to a geographically remote data center is still in place but takes the form of online, real-time mirroring to an alternate data center facility or private or public cloud environment, rather than to physical tape and/or offline media.

People Opportunities

This category relates to opportunities to increase the efficiency of the control environment through people or organizational means (i.e. control agent, organization, or operational changes). This undertaking is the least intuitive of the three areas but is a productive exercise to perform periodically. The objective is to analyze aspects of a control or set of related controls (for which control design has been validated by the process described above) and determine by whom and how the control activity should be performed. This task requires several steps, as follows:

Step 1: Analyze control execution and determine performance (quality) and efficiency (cost) factors. Attempt to value, or at least prioritize, their impact.

Step 2: Once you have determined the important factors to maximize and have assigned a value or at least a priority ranking of their impact on control performance (execution or efficiency), you can then analyze how to apply these performance and efficiency factors by determining the best assignment (i.e. who should perform the control) and how (applying the efficiency factors well).

Step 3: After identifying the factors and the priority ranking in **Step 2** consider whether revisions to the control assignment or execution can improve the performance or efficiency of the control(s). If so, apply those revisions to the assignment or execution of the control(s).

Step 4: Attempt to estimate the cost reduction that will result from these adjustments. Also try to estimate any other impacts of the revision, such as increased costs or benefits of the reassignment. To evaluate the impact of these changes, it is important to think broadly. Some financial impacts may include the following:

> » Value of improved control performance, if applicable.
> » Additional cost or savings associated with the reassignment of the control from a payroll/effort standpoint.
> » Impact of execution efficiency such as quicker or slower speed, taking into consideration the point regarding payroll costs and differential.
> » Factor in opportunity costs, if any. The reassignment of a control task will typically involve a benefit for the individual relieved of the responsibility and a cost for the individual taking on the task, the net cost/benefit of which needs to be considered. Keep in mind that the "opportunity cost" concept comes into play only when, after effecting the change, there is no availability (or "slack") in the respective individual's schedule. If there is slack in the individual's

schedule, there will be no tradeoff associated with the change. (I.e. "If I take this new control responsibility on, I can no longer do X": we need to estimate the reduction in value from not doing X into our analysis.)

» Consider other non-control related impacts. For example, in addition to the opportunity cost described above, the removal of a control from one group or process and re-assignment to another may have some broader impact, positively or negatively, on the group or process beyond the opportunity costs of the ceding and assuming party's time, described in the bullet above, (for example, impact on employee morale).

Some other Factors to Consider for People-Related Control Rationalization

This exercise should take into account other performance attributes of the agent, role or group performing the control, such as the following:

- Authority – The perceived authority of the control agent(s) that performs the control may improve adherence among those who must comply with the policies a control is enforcing.
- Knowledge and Professional Judgment – These factors are important characteristics of the control agent when the subject matter of the control is more complex.
- Motivation/Psychology – It is important to assign control(s) to someone or a group that has a good attitude and motivation as it relates to the performance of the control. For example, it may not be wise to task an individual who is chronically late or absent with reviewing other employees' attendance or time sheets.
- End-to-End Understanding of Related Process – Some controls demand an in-depth understanding of the overall process, requiring someone who has experience or understands the overall process intimately.

- Cost – Consider the control agent's or group's compensation level. With other things being equal, you would rather have lower-cost workers performing controls.
- Availability – Workers who have the "bandwidth" to take on the task are more likely to execute the control well and quickly. It also reduces or eliminates the opportunity costs that may reduce the benefit realized.
- Reducing Errors or Omissions – Again, with other factors being equal, someone who has the ability to perform the control correctly without error will generally perform the control better.

The efficiency dimensions of execution include all the factors of control execution that may have a financial impact, such as these:

- Conditions under which execution can occur most quickly or require the least resources
- Fitting into an existing workflow process, as opposed to creating a new process to accommodate the control(s) may be preferable (depending on the circumstances).
- Earlier detection of exceptions can reduce the impact or the cost of correcting or reversing them.
- Streamlining, Dovetailing – Insertion of control execution into naturally occurring processes with the least interruption.
- Performing the control at a time and place when all needed tools and reference material or data are readily available and accessible.

Technology-Related Opportunities

Factoring technology into the control rationalization process is generally easier than the Performance and Efficiency considerations outlined above. In this area, you simply want to analyze the current control execution and technology involved and look for opportunities to improve the efficiency and effectiveness of the control by better deploying technology. There are several ways in which technology can be leveraged to rationalize controls[10], including the following:

1. Automating – Refers to the process of evaluating the steps in the current control execution and looking for opportunities to automate some of the remaining manual steps. The analysis needs to estimate the NPV value of the benefit in terms of reduced control execution costs as well as the initial cost of configuration or developing a revised tool.

2. Optimizing – Optimizing entails evaluating technology alternatives that can be deployed to execute the control and choosing the best alternative.[11]

3. Standardizing – Standardizing is perhaps the most overlooked alternative for technology rationalization; nonetheless, there are often several opportunities to standardize the technology and tools used to perform a control. Doing so can yield significant efficiency and effectiveness benefits. The key is to look for the same control operated using different tools and software within the organization. Whenever this situation exists, the control execution will generally improve if one tool is used rather than performing the control over several different technology platforms.[12] The benefit is twofold. First, one of the

---

10 While this analysis and recommendation focuses on financial analysis in the context of improving risk-and-control decision making, the technology-related recommendations offered here are not unique to risk and controls and apply generally.

11 Generally this will be focused on choosing from technology offerings already licensed or available, as the financial benefit from control rationalization alone, although plausible, is rarely sufficient to justify the purchase of new software.

12 This does not mean, however, that the overall processing of the systems and the larger processes and functions consigned to the processing by these respective systems will improve. These impacts need to be considered as well. There may be good reasons why the two systems are employed and the current allotment of processing among the various systems is optimal; these factors go beyond consideration of the control(s) performance alone.

two (or more) processes in place will be superior and perform the control better or more efficiently than the others. The second benefit is realized from the economies of scale that result from pooling the transaction population and applying a standard and uniform process and technology to its process-ing and control execution. An example is a company that uses more than one software utility or application to document and process information technology change-management requests. While each application may be equally good, having two tools involved in this standard and routine control-related process-ing may introduce inefficiency and a higher risk of error, for several reasons. [13]

As you can see, there are many factors to consider in the periodic control rationalization process, a few of which were outlined above. The important point is that organizations tend to grow a complex and cumbersome or less efficient control estate over time and, once acquired, an organization will rarely step back to analyze their control environment from an efficiency and redundancy standpoint. For this reason, it is important to periodically assess the organization's overall control estate from a financial efficiency standpoint

---

13 Please note that while we are focusing on the control execution here, the analysis needs to incorporate the other effects of this change. It is possible (likely, in fact) that the overall financial assessment will overwhelm the impact of the control change, either increasing the benefit or reducing it. While the control rationalization may be the impetus for the change, the benefits may be much larger than the estimate for the control.

Closing Thoughts

This book has presented a fair amount of material and has done so in a somewhat cursory manner. Some of it was presented in a quasi-textbook fashion. The remaining material included general observations and recommendations that included a few illustrative examples. This work is not intended to suggest a false sense of precision or potential benefit to using financial analysis to improve the decision-making of the risk-and-control professional; nor is it intended to propose or provide the underpinning for implementing a rigid or methodical application of the recommendations and methods put forward for consideration. The intention of this work is simply this--first, to make the case to that reader that, (with the possible exception of the vague and uninstructive notion of "risk appetite"), (a) financial analysis has been largely omitted from current practice in the profession and (b) the use of financial analysis should be considered to improve decision making related to increasing the financial efficiency and effectiveness of an organization's control environment. The final objective was to suggest, in a straight forward and rudimentary fashion, some considerations and approaches that could be used to apply financial analysis to decision making of the risk-and-control profession in a consistent and defendable manner. I hope the reader will deem this dissertation to have been successful in meeting those modest goals. If not, maybe this text will succeed in encouraging a more serious treatment of this important subject matter.

In closing, this text has covered an important and largely neglected topic in a brief manner. This was done intentionally to focus attention on this important topic and to have others (i.e., individuals possessing greater training and ability in financial analysis and/or the risk-and-control profession) critique, revise, and advance the subject matter. The primary objective of this work is to shed light on this overlooked aspect of the risk-and-control profession. I did this by establishing a fact that is intuitively understood by many in the profession—that the risk-and-control discipline has generally lain outside the realm of effective financial analysis. While there are many reasons for this, I have asserted that it is unwise, given the costs involved in the design, implementation, operation, and assessment of controls. To further the analysis, I have proposed a definition of controls that is both simple and robust and, most importantly, lends itself to basic financial analysis. Next, this text explored the unique characteristics of general risk exposures and the controls to mitigate those risks that should be taken into account in devising a framework for the economic analysis of controls and applying appropriate financial analysis methods. With this foundation, a rudimentary framework was proposed to analyze controls from a financial standpoint that should be considered in the design, implementation, and operation of controls. After outlining this framework, the work explored the high-level implications of control design and operation that our financial analysis framework indicates. These factors include the cost drivers for control design and operation and the methods for estimating the benefit in terms of reduced residual risk exposure that results from the implementation and operating effectiveness of controls. Lastly, the text outlined some basic assertions and guidelines regarding methods to effect an economically efficient control environment for organizations based on the financial analysis framework proposed.

As a final point, it is understood that the primary focus of the control professional and organizations should be on assessment of risk and the design, implementation, and operation of controls to reduce the identified risk exposures to an acceptable level. This should take precedence, and the financial analysis of controls should be secondary to that primary focus of the control professional. That said, it is also true that organizations and control professionals should incorporate financial analysis into their work more, to effect control environments that are both effective *and* cost-efficient, as currently, the focus on cost-efficiency seems to be lacking in the profession.

Epilogue

I hope this book was helpful to you. It is a compilation of my practical experience and the impressions formed over more than twenty-five years working in the risk-and-control profession as well as my training in economics, finance, and accounting. You may notice this work has no bibliographic references citing other works, as I have not referenced any specific texts or other works in authoring this dissertation. I have simply organized my thoughts and drafted this work based on the experiences and observations garnered from working in the profession and applying basic financial concepts and analysis to the context of risk-and-control decision making. Similarity to any prior work—and I am not aware of any, although I would not be surprised if there were—is coincidental and a reflection of the fact that the underlying concepts presented in this text are commonly understood and accepted principles applied to the risk-and-control subject. This analysis was drawn solely from my own experience and views formed during a lengthy career in the risk-and-control profession in combination with the study of financial analysis and management decision-making gained through post-graduate study at Cornell University's Samuel Curtis Johnson Graduate School of Management, (where my daughter, Jessica Lynn Smith, is enrolled, as of the time of this publication).

I encourage the reader to correct or clarify any errors in this text and, in general, to expand on the study of this subject. If this book is useful to any reader in evaluating and improving their organization's control environment from a financial standpoint, it will have been well worth the effort.

www.ingramcontent.com/pod-product-compliance
Lightning Source LLC
Chambersburg PA
CBHW071630170526
45166CB00003B/1272